LET'S DISCOVER

A STUART HOUSE

Ruth Thomson

WATTS BOOKS

LONDON • NEW YORK • SYDNEY

© 1993 Watts Books
This edition 1995

Watts Books
96 Leonard Street
London
EC2A 4RH

Franklin Watts Australia
14 Mars Road
Lane Cove
NSW 2066

UK ISBN: 0 7496 1368 8

Dewey Decimal Classification Number 728

A CIP catalogue record for this book is available
from the British Library.

Editor: Sarah Ridley
Designer: Janet Watson
Photographer: Chris Fairclough
Picture researcher: Sarah Moule
Consultant: Robin Harcourt Williams,
archivist, Hatfield House.

Acknowledgements: the author and publishers
wish to thank Colonel Douglas McCord,
Curator, and Jenny Dean, guide, at Hatfield
House; Peter Lary, Cathy Hagan, Annette
Tickner, Keith Ramtahal, Suzanne Littler, Carol
Nottage, Kim Nottage, Debbie Dixon, Sharon
McInerney, Hugo Le Conte and pupils of
Sapphire Class at Hargrave Park School,
Islington; and Charles Bradley, for all their help
with this publication.

Additional photographs: Ancient Art and
Architecture Library 29b; Bridgeman Art
Library 17b, 21b, 23tl, 28br, 30b; Devonshire
Collection, Chatsworth (reproduced by permis-
sion of the Chatsworth Settlement Trustees)
15b; English Heritage 15tc; Mary Evans Picture
Library 28-29t; Michael Holford 8-9b, 9tl, 15t,
15c; Fotomas Index/Hatfield House 27bl; thanks
to the Marquess of Salisbury, Hatfield House
cover cl, 4, 6t, 11t, 11c, 16, 18tr, 19tr, 30t; S & O
Mathews 9tr, 9cr; National Trust Photographic
Library 21tr, 28bl; National Trust Photographic
Library/John Bethell 23cr; Unichrome 25b.

Printed in Malaysia

Contents

The first Stuart king

For over a hundred years, from 1485, the powerful Tudor family ruled England. Queen Elizabeth I, the last Tudor ruler, was on the throne for almost fifty years. She died in 1603, having never married and with no children to succeed her.

The crown passed to a new family of rulers — the Stuarts. King James VI of Scotland, son of Mary Queen of Scots and cousin of Queen Elizabeth I, became King James I of England.

James I took on many problems from his cousin Elizabeth when he was crowned in 1603. He added to them by falling out with Parliament over the power of the king. He believed that he was king by God's will. He thought he could rule and spend money however he wished, without any interference from Parliament.

He spent only a small part of the year governing from his palace in London. He far preferred to spend his time hunting, either on his own country estates or on those of his rich followers. He and his wife entertained extravagantly, regularly holding lavish banquets and costumed spectacles, called masques.

A portrait of James I. He always wore padded clothes, because he feared he might be assassinated by his enemies.

? LET'S INVESTIGATE

Looking carefully at the family tree, can you answer these questions?

- Who was Queen Elizabeth's grandfather?
- Who was Edward VI's mother ?
- Who was Henry VIII's fourth wife?

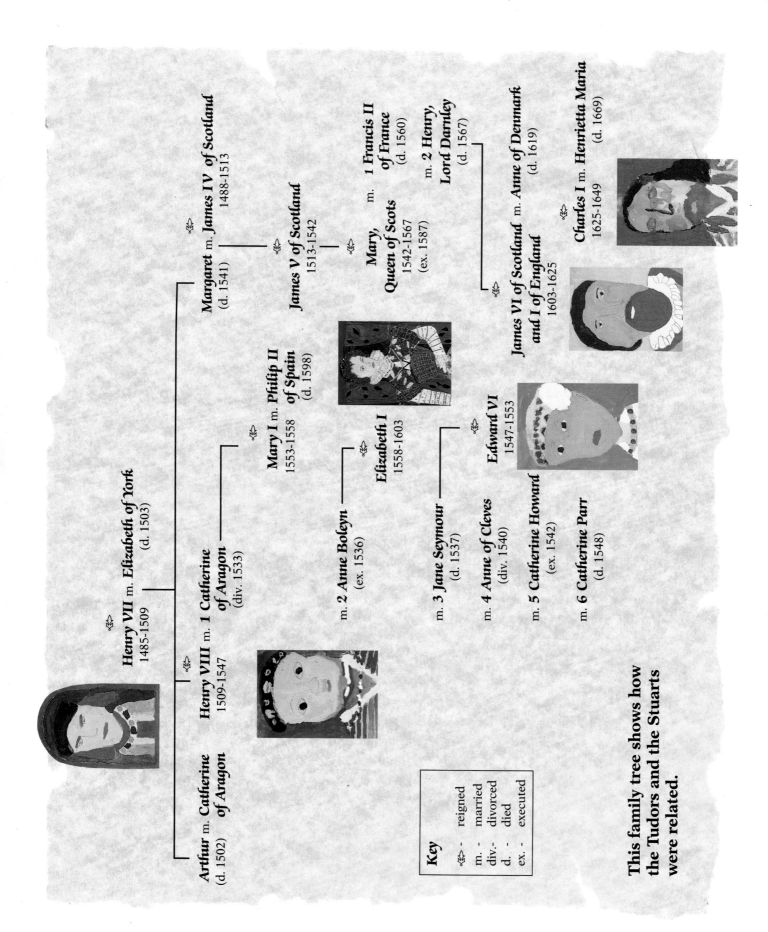

Henry VII m. *Elizabeth of York*
1485-1509   (d. 1503)

Arthur m. *Catherine of Aragon*
(d. 1502)

Henry VIII m. 1 *Catherine of Aragon*
1509-1547   (div. 1533)

m. 2 *Anne Boleyn*
(ex. 1536)

m. 3 *Jane Seymour*
(d. 1537)

m. 4 *Anne of Cleves*
(div. 1540)

m. 5 *Catherine Howard*
(ex. 1542)

m. 6 *Catherine Parr*
(d. 1548)

Mary I m. *Philip II of Spain*
1553-1558   (d. 1598)

Elizabeth I
1558-1603

Edward VI
1547-1553

Margaret m. *James IV of Scotland*
(d. 1541)   1488-1513

James V of Scotland
1513-1542

Mary, m.
Queen of Scots
1542-1567
(ex. 1587)

1 *Francis II of France*
(d. 1560)

m. 2 *Henry, Lord Darnley*
(d. 1567)

James VI of Scotland m. *Anne of Denmark*
and I of England   (d. 1619)
1603-1625

Charles I m. *Henrietta Maria*
1625-1649   (d. 1669)

Key

&> - reigned
m. - married
div.- divorced
d. - died
ex. - executed

This family tree shows how the Tudors and the Stuarts were related.

People and their dress

Society in Stuart times was divided into four main groups — the nobles at court, the citizens and merchants who lived in towns, the landowning farmers, known as yeomen, and the landless poor.

It was clear from the clothes people wore what their position was in society. People at court set the fashion, wearing expensive clothes to display the importance of their position. They wore brocaded or embroidered clothes of silk or satin, decorated with frills and lace.

Farmworkers wore hard wearing leather or woollen breeches (short trousers), a linen shirt and a long jacket. The women wore plain linen dresses.

Clothes were all hand-sewn and time-consuming to make. Poorer people handed their clothes down to members of their family.

Elizabeth I wore spectacular bejewelled and embroidered dresses edged with fine lace. They dazzled her subjects and emphasised her power.

? LET'S INVESTIGATE

Find out what these garments are:-

- hose
- doublet
- garters
- jerkin
- breeches
- French roll.

Look at pictures and books to find out more about costumes of the time.

Both men and women wore ruffs made of fine cotton, starched to make them stiff.

Fashionable collars like this were supported on a wire frame.

Shoes were made of soft leather or silk brocade. Make a pair of your own from felt.

Women wore enormous hooped petticoats, called farthingales, under their skirts. Draw your own pictures of Stuart costumes and label them.

Houses of the time

James I gave important, well-paid posts to his favourites and sold titles and Crown land to courtiers who flattered him.

Many courtiers spent their new-found wealth building houses. They wanted to remain in favour with the king and expected him to visit them. They built houses with rooms for themselves and also with a series of State Rooms, fit for the king to use.

The owners built their houses in the latest fashionable style. The buildings were symmetrical, highly decorated and had large windows. This style of building is known as Jacobean.

The homes of the poor were very different. They lived in wretched hovels, with only one room in which the whole family lived, ate and slept. These houses were smoky, draughty, dark and smelly. They had no chimneys and no glass in the small windows.

Make your own model house out of card or clay.

? LET'S INVESTIGATE

Are there any Jacobean houses in your area? Manor houses sometimes have a date written over the door (Jacobean houses date between 1603 and 1625). What materials are they built from? Is it possible to find these materials locally?

Town houses were often huddled close together in narrow streets. Many were built of timber with walls of plaster.

Merchants and yeomen farmers lived in houses with up to a dozen rooms, as well as out-buildings. These were usually made from local materials, because transport was so difficult and expensive on the bad roads of the time.

The poor lived in houses like this. Pairs of curved timbers, called crucks, support the roof.

Audley End, built by the Earl of Suffolk, was one of the largest houses ever built in England. It was started in 1603. By 1614, when the Earl became Lord Treasurer, it had already cost him a fortune. He used public money to continue paying for the work. When he was found out, he lost his job and was tried for embezzlement.

Hatfield House

In 1496, the Bishop of Ely built himself a palace at Hatfield. It was a square building round a courtyard. When Henry VIII made himself head of the Church of England, he confiscated the palace from the Church, and sent his children, Prince Edward and Princess Elizabeth to live there.

James I inherited Hatfield when he became king, but the palace was not to his taste. He forced Robert Cecil, his chief minister, to give up his own luxurious house, called Theobalds, in exchange for the palace.

The palace walls are simply decorated with brick patterns.

The remaining wing of the Old Palace.

The front of Hatfield House. This was only one of the three grand houses which Cecil had built. Hatfield is still owned by the Cecil family.

Robert Cecil demolished three sides of the palace and used the rubble for the foundations of a new house, which took five years to build. He was exceedingly wealthy from his posts at court and could afford to build on a very grand scale.

Robert Cecil's portrait

The ornate stone facade emphasised Cecil's wealth.

The builders used local wood and bricks, but stone was shipped, at great expense, from Kent and from Caen in Normandy. Marble for the fireplaces and the floor of the Great Hall was brought from Italy. Famous craftsmen from Holland, France and England fitted out the interior.

Looking at the details

The Old Palace and Hatfield House were built 100 years apart. If you look closely at the details of the buildings, you can see how styles changed.

The red bricks and sloping roof tiles of the palace look very humble compared with the richness of the decoration of the house. The style of stonework was influenced by the Italian Renaissance. Renaissance means rebirth, and this was a time when the Italians started to re-use the ancient Roman style of architecture.

Before you go into a grand house, take a look at the outside details of the windows, doors and chimneys. These can give you clues about when the house might have been built.

The Old Palace has only a few chimneys, but Hatfield House has several long lines of them. These displayed to the outside world how rich Cecil was to have so many fireplaces and to be able to afford so much fuel.

The windows in the palace are smaller than those in the house and have small diagonal-shaped panes. By the 1600s, glass had become much cheaper and easier to use. Stone surrounds can bear more weight than brick ones, so these windows are far bigger.

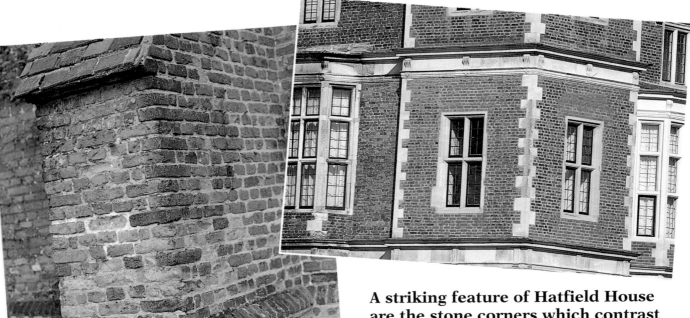

A striking feature of Hatfield House are the stone corners which contrast with the brick. These emphasise the shape of the building. Compare them with the brick corners of the old palace.

The Great Hall

The Great Hall at Hatfield, in common with many great halls, has panelled walls, a decorated ceiling, a minstrel's gallery and an enormous fireplace.

The centre of a grand house was its impressive great hall. Visitors would have been ushered in to wait their turn to see the lord. The whole household, often 60 to 80 people, ate their main meal here every day and, from time to time, the lord would entertain guests with enormous feasts. He sat under a canopy at a high table, his guests on either side and the rest of the household in front.

Feasts were lavish affairs, lasting for hours. As many as 32 different dishes were provided. People chose which dishes they wanted to eat. There were huge joints of beef, venison and lamb, as well as several sorts of fish. For those who preferred fowl, there was often a choice of lark, turkey, swan, quail or goose. The meat was accompanied by vegetables and salads.

People cut their meat with a knife and ate with their hands, using a spoon to scoop up the juices.

Forks, recently introduced from Italy, were still a rarity, except in the most fashionable houses.

A costume for a masque, by Inigo Jones, who was a famous architect.

After the main courses, the lord would retire to the withdrawing room with his guests, for a banquet of sweetmeats, such as marzipan, tarts, pies and fruit.

Meanwhile, the servants would clear the hall and move the tables away in preparation for the entertainment. There was always music and sometimes dancing or the performance of a masque.

The Long Gallery

On the upper floor were the king and queen's withdrawing rooms and bedrooms, linked by a long gallery. This was a narrow but long room with scarcely any furniture and numerous windows overlooking the gardens below.

In cold or wet weather, people passed the time by walking up and down the gallery, chatting and admiring the portraits of famous people that hung on the walls. These portraits were rather like the signed photographs of famous people today.

The Long Gallery at Hatfield House has been filled with furniture from the 18th century. In Robert Cecil's day, there would only have been a few chairs along the walls.

Here too, noblemen could practise their swordplay or while away their time playing games, such as shovel board, backgammon or draughts. The Jacobeans were also keen gamblers and played dice and card games, such as cribbage and whist.

Make your own portrait of a famous Elizabethan or Jacobean person. This is a collage of Elizabeth I.

Shovel board is similar to shove ha'penny. Make your own board out of stiff card. Divide it into 12 sections, each just wider than a 1p coin. Hit coins on to the board with the side of your palm. Score a point every time a coin lands without touching any lines.

A backgammon board from Jacobean times.

The interior

Everything in a grand house was richly decorated. Not a single surface was left plain. The plaster ceilings were ribbed and patterned, the walls were panelled with wood and hung with tapestries or pictures. The state rooms had large, imposing chimney pieces, made of marble or carved wood.

The newel posts were richly carved and topped with animals.

A magnificent wooden staircase was one of the main features of the house, designed to impress visitors.

The plaster design on this ceiling is known as strapwork. It was originally all white.

18

Portraits of famous
people hung on the walls.

The lifesize sculpture over this
fireplace in the King's Great Chamber
is of James I. It was placed there to
flatter the king, should he ever visit.

The family coat of arms was
displayed in the Great Hall,
to remind everyone who saw
it of the family's importance.

?

LET'S INVESTIGATE

Look out for coats of arms in
portraits, on gates and doorways
and stained glass windows. Make
drawings of them. Find out about
the colours and patterns that have
been used.

The furniture

Even in grand houses, such as Hatfield, there was not a great deal of furniture. Most of it was of oak and was huge and solid.

The Great Hall had several long tables, but very few chairs. Chairs were used only by the master and mistress of the house and important guests. Everyone else sat on stools or benches.

Household goods and clothes were stored either in wooden chests or in cupboards.

The table in the Great Hall at Hatfield is 7 metres long and 1 metre wide. It is made of oak.

Babies slept in wooden rocking cradles. This was King Charles I's cradle.

This is called a farthingale chair. It has a high back and no arms, so a woman wearing a farthingale (see page 7) could sit down on it comfortably.

The four-poster bed was the most valuable piece of furniture. It often had an elaborately carved headboard and pillars with heavy curtains hanging down. The sleeper lay on a feather mattress on top of a straw-filled sack. The curtains were shut at night for privacy and to keep in warmth. This one at Knole was made for James II in 1685.

Chests were often carved on the front and sides. They sometimes doubled as seats.

Keeping clean

Even the grandest houses had no running water or lavatories. Servants carried every drop of water in and out of the houses in buckets. At Hatfield House, the water came from a spring close to the house.

People did not consider it necessary to wash every day, although they did wash their hands at table, before meals. Elizabeth I is said to have washed once a fortnight and James I less often than that!

During Elizabeth I's reign, Sir John Harrington invented a flushing lavatory, but it did not become popular. In big houses, most people used a close-stool — a chamber pot inside a box with a padded seat — which could be moved about. At Hatfield, the servants slept with the close-stools near at hand and took them into the bedchambers when called for.

In the 1600s, there were several outbreaks of plagues. People believed that if their houses smelled sweet and fresh, it might help ward off the disease. Pomanders and bowls of pot pourri or dried lavender were put in rooms to make them smell better. Women often carried posies of fresh flowers to sniff.

Lavender and roses for making pot pourri were grown in the garden. The flowers were stripped and dried. The rose petals were mixed with aromatic spices.

The servants used hidden back stairs to fetch and carry. The door to the stairs is disguised by panelling.

This close-stool can be found at Knole, in Kent.

A basin and ewer were put on the table for diners to wash their hands before eating.

Make your own pomander. Push whole cloves into a fresh orange, covering it completely. Leave it for a week in a warm place to dry slowly.

? LET'S INVESTIGATE

In 1665, the Great Plague killed almost 70,000 Londoners. Find out what caused it and what people did to try to prevent it from spreading.

The gardens

The pleasure gardens which surrounded a big house were as spectacular and sumptuous as the house itself.

No expense was spared. There were terraces and lawns, a rose garden, scented flowerbeds, a knot garden, fountains and a lake. For amusement, there was a maze and a bowling green. Fruit trees and climbing roses were trained against sunny walls. On the top of

Knot gardens were made with low, clipped shrubs, planted to make a geometric pattern. They were designed to be looked down on from a height. This modern one at Hatfield has been grown only with plants known in the 16th and 17th centuries.

raised mounts of earth were shaded seats and banqueting houses, where people ate sweet dishes and drank wine.

Robert Cecil employed John Tradescant, a famous botanist, to plant the garden at Hatfield, and sent him to France, Italy and Belgium to collect rare plants. He brought back figs, tulip bulbs, lilies, anemones, myrtles and rare roses.

This is the only mulberry tree left of the four that James I is said to have planted at Hatfield. He tried to promote the growing of mulberry trees in England, because he was keen to start a silk industry. Mulberry leaves are the favourite food of silkworms.

The Hatfield gardens spread in every direction around the house. Grand avenues of trees lead from the entrances of the park to the house.

25

The parkland

Beyond the gardens stretched an enormous park and farmlands, which provided the large household with almost all its needs. The forest gave wood for building, fencing and fuel. Cows and sheep were kept for leather and wool as well as meat, and were killed in a slaughterhouse in the grounds. Some of the meat was salted or potted for the winter.

Vegetables, such as onions, cabbages, carrots and peas were grown in the kitchen garden. Herbs were grown both for seasoning and for medical remedies.

Apples, pears, plums, cherries and figs were grown in the orchard. Bees were kept in straw hives under the trees for their honey, since sugar was not readily available.

A park-keeper was in charge of the outdoor workers. A huntsman caught deer. A falconer trained hawks and eagles to catch birds such as partridges, quails and pigeons.

A fisherman provided the house with eels, trout, carp and pike from the nearby river. A keeper of spaniels trained the dogs to catch waterbirds, such as snipe, bittern and herons, which were regular delicacies at banquets.

These two great oak trees, known as 'Sentinels', are almost five hundred years old. They guard the entrance to the ancient deer park at Hatfield.

It was under an oak tree in Hatfield's park that Elizabeth I learned she was to be queen. That tree is no longer there, but Queen Elizabeth II planted a replacement.

Robert Cecil employed two French gardeners to start a vineyard. Thirty thousand vines were planted but the vineyard was abandoned before any wine was produced. Only the wall that once surrounded it now remains.

Noblemen regularly came to Hatfield for stag-hunting and hawking.

The river Lea runs through the parkland. Robert Cecil widened this part to make an ornamental lake.

Preparing food

Most of the cooking was done in the kitchen, over an open coal fire in an enormous fireplace, where food was either boiled or roasted.

Joints of meat were roasted for hours on long iron spits, which were turned from time to time. The fat was caught in a long pan underneath.

Stews, vegetables and puddings were boiled in enormous iron cauldrons, which hung from a hook over the fire.

Pies and cakes were made in a nearby room called a pastry. There were separate out-buildings for baking, brewing ale, making butter and cheese and storing food and wine.

The main meal of the day was dinner, eaten at midday. It consisted of two or three courses, finishing with sweetmeats, cheese and fruit.

A seventeenth century kitchen showing how the spit was turned.

Rich families used plates and drinking vessels of silver and pewter.

28

Herbs and spices were crushed in a mortar and pestle.

Knot biscuits

Ingredients	Equipment
40g margarine	• *mixing bowl*
100g caster sugar	• *wooden spoon*
2 eggs	• *teaspoon*
1 tsp cinnamon	• *egg whisk*
1 tsp caraway seeds	• *knife*
1 tsp mace	• *baking tray*
225g self-raising flour	*(greased)*

Set the oven at 350⁰ F (180⁰ C)

1 Cream the margarine and sugar.
2 Beat the eggs and stir them in.
3 Mix in the spices all together.
4 Fold in the sieved flour to make a smooth, stiff dough.
5 Form the dough into long rolls.
6 Knot or plait them.
7 Bake the knots for 15 minutes.
8 Put them on a wire tray to cool.

The chapel

Great houses usually had their own chapel and a priest who would conduct services for the family and their servants.

James I ordered scholars to make a new English translation of the Bible. It was printed in 1611. It became the standard Bible for almost 300 years and is still in print. James believed that only the Established Church should be allowed to exist. This upset both the Roman Catholics and the Puritans, who were not allowed to set up their own churches as they wished.

Roman Catholics, forced to worship in secret, plotted in 1605 to blow up the Houses of Parliament. Robert Cecil sent soldiers to search the cellars and found Guy Fawkes with barrels of gunpowder. Fawkes and the other plotters were all hanged.

The stained glass windows in the Hatfield House chapel show twelve biblical stories.

? LET'S INVESTIGATE

In 1620, a group of Puritans sailed in the Mayflower from England to America. Find out why they went and what happened to them once they arrived.

Puritans believed in leading a simple life and doing good works. In contrast to the fine clothes of the rich, they wore plain clothes with simple collars.

Places to visit

- **Aston Hall,** Birmingham, West Midlands.
Built between 1618 and 1635.

- **Audley End,** near Saffron Waldron, Essex.
Built for the Sir Thomas Howard, Lord Treasurer to James I, between 1603 and 1616.

- **Blickling Hall,** near Aylsham, Norfolk.
Built for Sir Henry Hobart, Chief Justice of the Common Pleas, between 1619 and 1622.

- **Burton Agnes Hall,** near Bridlington, Humberside.
Built between 1598 and 1610, for Sir Henry Griffiths.

- **Charlton Park House,** Malmesbury, Wiltshire.
Built for the Earls of Suffolk, 1607.

- **Chastleton House,** near Moreton in Marsh, Oxfordshire.
Built about 1603 for Walter Johns, a wool merchant.

- **Cranborne Manor Gardens,** Cranborne, Wimborne, Dorset.
Includes a herb garden, Jacobean mount and knot garden planted with old-fashioned flowers.

- **Doddington Hall,** Doddington, Lincolnshire.
Completed in 1600.

- **Dorfold Hall,** Nantwich, Cheshire.
Built 1616.

- **Ham House,** Ham, Surrey.
Originally built in 1610, for Sir Thomas Vavassour, Knight Marshal to James I. Altered in the 1670s.

- **Hardwick Hall,** Derbyshire.
Built for Elizabeth, Countess of Shrewsbury, better known as Bess of Hardwick, in 1590, and still not finished at the time of her death in 1608. The least altered of all Elizabethan houses.

- **Knole,** Sevenoaks, Kent.
Rebuilt for the Earl of Dorset, between 1604 and 1608.

- **Levens Hall,** Kendal, Cumbria.
Built for the Bagot family. Contains Jacobean furniture.

- **Montacute House,** Yeovil, Somerset.
Built in 1598 for Sir Edward Phelips, a lawyer, later Speaker in the House of Commons and Master of the Rolls.

- **Plas Teg,** Pontblyddyn, near Mold, Wales.
Built in 1610. It has an exceptional carved oak staircase.

- **Sherborne Castle,** Sherborne, Dorset.
Built by Sir Walter Raleigh in 1594 and enlarged in 1625 by the Earl of Bristol.

- **Thrumpton Hall,** Nottingham.
House built in 1607 incorporating an earlier manor house.

- **Wollaton Hall,** Nottingham.
Begun in 1580 for Sir Francis Willoughby.

Index